Dear

poetry

Love, Sheila

we make the air

we make the air

the poetry of
Lina Chartrand

TLC Press
1998

Poetry © Kye Marshall, 1998
All rights reserved

Edited by Maureen Hynes and Ingrid MacDonald
Text design by Ingrid MacDonald
Cover design by Martha Newbigging of flippix

Published by TLC Press, 1998
(established to produce *we make the air*)
c/o 128 Withrow Avenue, Toronto, Ontario, M4K 1C9

Distributed by University of Toronto Press

Cover art by Lina Chartrand, 1994
Cover photograph by Maureen Hynes
Photograph on page 60 by Marcia MacKinnon
Photograph on page 62 by Catherine Maunsell

Special thanks to: Kye Marshall; Martha Newbigging; Liz Ukrainetz; and Ann Decter of McGilligan Books for guidance and assistance; Jacinthe Michaud, Jane Springer and Susan Kealey for copy editing and translation.

Some of these poems appeared in
Contemporary Verse 2, Grain and *Pittsburgh Quarterly*.

Canadian Cataloguing in Publication Data

Chartrand, Lina, 1948-1994
    We make the air: the poetry of Lina Chartrand

Some poems in French.
ISBN 0-9684557-0-0

I. Hynes, Maureen. II. MacDonald, Ingrid, 1960- . III. Title.

PS8555.H43055W4 1998   C811'.54   C98-932735-3
PR9199.3.C42W4 1998

These people and organizations made this book possible:
Mary Louise Adams and Helen Humphreys; Kelley Aitken;
Suzanne Ballantyne; Betty Beaton; Jake and Carma Beerepoot;
Gay Bell and Donna Marchand; Don Bouzek; Linda Briskin;
Bob Miller Book Room; Wendy and Stuart Campbell;
Paul and Diane Caron; Léo Chartrand;
Maurice et Doreen Chartrand; Richard et Lorraine Chartrand;
John et Raymonde Chartrand Motil; Deborah Clipperton;
The Company of Sirens; Contemporary Verse 2;
Brian Conway; Mary Rose Cowan; Barbara Crisp;
Shawna Dempsey and Lorri Millan;
Directing, Acting and Writing for Camera Workshop;
Caroline Duetz and Charlene Roycht; Valerie Edwards and
Loretta Clark; Rita Fridella; Sandy Fox and Lynnie Johnston;
Cynthia Grant and Zöe Grant-Wilson; Marion Green;
John Greyson/Grey Zone; Gwyneth Griffith; Amanda Hale;
Sue Hartman and Leslie Nanos; Debra Henderson;
Dr. Alisa Hornung; Jude Johnston; Louis and Mariette Julien;
Annette La Barre; Diana Leblanc; Myra Lefkowitz and
Joanne Bacon; Jane Liddel and Pam Wedd;
Naomi Lechinsky; Donald and Marcia MacKinnon;
Mary Marshall; Philinda Masters and Susan Power;
Catherine Maunsell; Diana Meredith; Jacinthe Michaud;
Vivien Moore and Dave Wilson; Mary Jane Mossman;
Nicole Nash and the late Philip Nash; Sheri O'Rourke;
Rosamund Owen; Richard Partington; Helen Carmichael Porter;
Cheryl Proctor; Kyle Rae; C.T. Rowe; Rowesa; Ann Ruebottom;
Jennifer Rudder; Barbara Shainbaum; Susan Schellenberg;
Doreen Silvera; Diane Simard and Dave Broadfoot;
Tori Smith; Judy Stanleigh; Sheila Stewart;
Anne Stokes and Mary Ellen Mathison;
Susan Swan; Lisa Trudel; Betsy Trumpener; Liz Ukrainetz;
John Van Burek; Jacqueline and Lawrence Weston;
Marilyn Williams; Anthony Wilson; Barb Young; Eve Zaremba and
Ottie Lockey; and others who wish to remain anonymous.
Thank you.

Kye Marshall, Maureen Hynes, Ingrid MacDonald

Between our desire for absolute love and inability to love absolutely lies a great fear. When, despite this paradox, our desires do not die, it is a cause for celebration.

Entre notre désire d'un amour absolu et notre incapacité d'aimer absolument réside une grande peur. Lorsqu'en dépit de ce paradoxe, nos désirs ne périssent point, c'est un événement à célébrer.

Lina Chartrand

Contents

Meet desire

    Ma langue 10
    Sylvia 12
    Doctor Xiabo 13
    Paralysis 15
    Meet desire 17
    Affirmation 23
    A similée 24
    The counter 26
    O home on the range 27
    We make the air 28
    Dimanche après-midi 29

Horizons blurring

    Horizons blurring 32
    Shadow and clock 33
    A shady diagonal 35
    The Ordinary Hornby View 38
    Aristazabal 39

Dry-throated sky

    Les bras chauds 44
    Easter 48
    Dry-throated sky 49
    Grace 50
    After Supper 51
    Death song 52
    Brother 53
    Collect yourself 55
    The northern clinic 57
    Upon a Brother's Death 59

Afterword

    About Lina Chartrand
        by Brian Conway 60
    About Lina Chartrand's Poetry
        by Maureen Hynes 62

Meet desire

MA LANGUE

I make you guess as
I write *ma chérie*
in red mud on your
transparent blue skin.
N? A? Na? No. Maw?

No, my red mouth forms,
not maw. *Ma*, my, mine.
My *langue* sits tight on
your icy dry skin.
A fingernail slides,

accenting the e
in *chérie*, draws blood,
like a sliver or
a salty lick or
the stiff rope burning

two blue wrists crossed
behind your back. Hear my
confession, darling:
I tore off my dress,
gashed the oak table,

stomped on auntie's hat,
Paul pulled down my pants,
made me swallow dirt.
A wooden swing banged
his head, knocked him out

and horsey's head rocked
like a hammer, laughed.
A distant cello
rasps a reply. I
damn near cry out, break—

spit a sour breath
hot down your neck and

taste your wooden
choker; faded bead
letters spell out come

to me, *ma chérie*,
come.

SYLVIA

Serpentine branches
dive underground for
a secret embrace
in haste eleven
brown stories below
the room with the bed
made up before noon
please. I'm expecting
a guest, a woman.
She wishes to stay
at the Sylvia
upon English Bay.

Melon, raspberry
and crème caramel,
I lick my fingers,
slow suck an old taste
back to life at the
Hotel Sylvia
upon English Bay.

She tracks sea salt on
carpets, marble steps,
singular white trails
on black lacquered trays.
Arching her back
on pale sheets, yellow-
skirted orchids, red-
centred; odorous
freesia, violets,
gardenia bouquets,
the Sylvia sails
upon English Bay.

DOCTOR XIABO

Radar fingertips
on my wrist.
> Tongue please.

Green tea
from her kitchen
before treatment.

Xiabo says:
> many English words sound
> the same.
> Could you please explain.

> What is affection?

Like our talks,
friendship, I reply.
She gives me advice:
> Don't always wear black.

> What means tenderness?

Like Chinese herbs,
a warm potion
that heals the body.

> When we came here,
Xiabo says,
> my husband abandoned me.
> I walked three hours
> daughter small
> on my back,
> no money.

> What is passion?

Like acupressure
points. Deep.
Electric.
By the door
my discarded birkenstocks
make a face-down shelter
over her pretty shoes.

    Love?

Like acupuncture,
I think,
the pain of the needle
is the best cure.

PARALYSIS

Café rendez-vous
beckons me away
middle of the day,

a chance to escape
devilish despair.
Do I imagine

my friend's frown upon
my dishevelled hair?
Deux cafés aux lait

s'il vous plaît. Merci.
Watch her but don't look.
Talk but don't betray

the paralysis.
Stir coffee, gaze down,
gently nestle spoon

in saucer, closer
safer, clinging hard
to white cup. Now squeeze

index through handle;
breathe and breathe again.
Command fisted hand

to lift up the cup.
Part lips and swallow.
Again. One more time.

Cup empty. Cup drained.
Cup begins descent —
Do I discern her

eye in the bottom
of my cup? The eye
explodes the veneer

of my tight-lipped smile.
The eye approaches,
it climbs my tongue,

rides an ascending
breath, agitated,
alights, flutters, flees —

a cacophony,
Watch but don't look,
Talk but don't betray

the paralysis.
In darkness, await.
Grey curtain rises.

Head tilted, holding
empty cup to her
ear, she deciphers

lost conversations,
still-born, arrested;
she squints as she hears

china splintering.
Her impatient thumb
enters the bowl of

my spoon and presses
in vain, no, not in
vain, but she refrains

too soon. She gives up.

MEET DESIRE

Meet desire
at the train station
a woman in a hat
silk stockings good shoes.
She descends the portable step.
The conductor offers his arm,
admires her unwrinkled tailored suit,
the ribbon at the neck
of her frilly white blouse.
She carries a square blue overnight bag
    (bottles,
    a compact for colour and definition,
    eau de cologne in a crystal atomizer).

You know why she has come.
You have no reason to disappoint her.

In her elegant leather attaché case
    (good paper,
    fountain pen,
    blotter)
she has your name on a list.

Her red fingernail runs down the black print in
                            the phone book.

You feel her approach:
a craving for chocolate,
unremarkable at first,
outdoors a whiff of Gitanes,
a hot palm burns the back of your neck.

She visits only those with imagination
(ten naked nuns, you said it).

*

She's looking for you all over town.
You know it and she knows it so why be afraid?
    (Because you need to write with rhythm,
    count syllables,
    be specific metaphoric poetic.)
Let it stretch out
lie around
sloppy shirt-tail sticking out
laundry basket full
shelves dusty
let desire be un-nice
hairy smelly wet muddy
a bed gritty with toast crumbs and cigarette ash
untucked sheets
twisted heaps of underwear knotted in balls
a grey and yellow-stained mattress on the floor
moldy coffee cups
amid turps and brushes.

A moon shines onto your hand, calls a voice:
"You'll lose your shape without a corset and a
                              good brassiere."

Bra-zeer.

*

Your body spread, hung, draped itself on his body,
you inhaled his smoke,
his whiskey kisses.
You rode in his car on a sticky afternoon,
found the melting licorice in the glove compartment.
He let you open the gum, the mints.
Your crinoline crisp on your legs.

        (The chrome buttons and dials on the dash
                      like a rocket ship,

>   shining Brylcreem hair, cuff links,
>   thick gold band on his finger,
>   the steering wheel, the stick shift.)

The stick shift.
You hated his girlfriend:
>   her kitchen a high gloss turquoise,
>   square corners,
>   polished toaster and kettle.

Your white sailor's hat perky on your head,
you sat on his lap.

They wouldn't let you go in his car any more
so you sneaked into his room,
his roomer's room,
the salty clothes smell,
dirty kleenexes under the bed,
loose change in a jar under the bureau,
a zippered black leather brush case.

*

Desire has a leather case,
cute manicure set with sky blue baby blue
>   mother of pearl handles,
fake but nice.

*

Scene at the theatre:
"Where do I plug in the kettle?" you ask her.
"Backstage," she replies.
You interrupt the show, soft-shoe across the
>   scene.
"Oh, excuse me, don't mind me..."
Ah! The curtain comes down for intermission.
"Can I make anyone else some tea?" (You feel
>   stupid.)

*

You pose as a woman with intelligence,
the look on your face of a woman with
                          worthwhile thoughts.
A laugh escapes like a burp or a fart from inside
                                          you.

*

Scene in the living room:
"You have to go now," you tell her.
"It's too late to start an interesting conversation.
The taxi will be here any minute."

*

She stretches out beneath your skin
her paws reaching into your shoulder blades
ribs interlocking with yours
snout stinky in your throat
mons veneris pressing you
her heart confusing your blood
losing
its rhythm combusts.

Running.
Chased by desire.
Can't sleep.

*

Living room again:
She puts her hand on yours.
You lie on the carpet.
You wait.
She's quiet.

You could make love but you won't.
You could make love but you won't.

*

As soon as desire steps off the train,
as soon as she is alone in her hotel room
she changes herself into a bear,
a cow, a dog,
it could be any of them.
Tonight a wild yellow cat with fangs and hips
                              arcs
invisibly swiftly from roof to roof searching
for girls with cat's eyes,
shine-in-the-dark eyes,
piercing-curious-questioning eyes.
She swoops into (right into) descends into
                        (deep) your body and you
are — you are —

"The tiger in the night isn't desire," she says.
                          "He is a man
chasing his vision of desire."

"Well, ex-cuse me."

"Long ago,
long-like-a-snake ago
(desire is of the earth, not the sky),
many earths ago, many skies ago,
the snake stretched its eagle wings,
flung itself around the planet,
sucked up its tail
and swallowed us awake."

*

You lie on the carpet together.
You might make love.
You might.

*

Desire's leaving town.
After sundown.
At the train station the air will be clear and cool.
She will sit in the waiting room.
She will cross her legs.
A loudspeaker voice will announce the next train.
She will put on her gloves.
No one will see her off.
She won't be leaving home or going home.
She'll keep travelling by train from town to town.
If she wants a change,
she'll visit a fine department store,
replace her shoes or her handbag,
buy a new shade of lipstick.
She'll always be a visitor,
always the guest.
If she fails in one town,
she'll get it right in the next.

*

The taxi driver knocks at your door.
She sleeps, she doesn't hear.
The street light shines through the window,
frames her arm resting on yours,
making an x in the square of light.
The taxi driver doesn't knock again.
He gives up, he drives away.

You know why she has come.
You have no reason to disappoint her.

AFFIRMATION

She wets the edges of a pie shell
a chain of half moons
kissed by an egg.

Her looking glass blinks
the planet of an eye.

She fists the air and
poof!
a crawl of crustaceans
to Casa Luna

la folie of *tout*
Paris, limey fever
for the *bal masque*

like any ball, a
final resurrection
of thieves.
A curve
of flaming organza
disappears. Midnight.
Big Ben smiles a yin yang face,
cat's eyes,
the Tao of London.

Courage, her empty life shot
full of aesthetics.

A SIMILÉE

I decide to let go of her dans le bain. It starts out like n'importe quel autre soir's routine de bain. We give our face a beauty treatment, un pouce de Noxzema, not rubbed in. Le bain's short chubby legs curl up & its sloping back invites nos épaules fatiguées. Notre corps entre dans le bain. We lean back & spread nos jambes apart. L'eau chaude s'empresse hors de la champlure. Notre corps nous dégoute. Lumps stick out de nos hanches inégales, our breasts droop & wrinkle, awful au toucher.

Our flabby thighs bob comme les baleines sur Lloyd Bridges Sea Hunt, blanches, glissantes, épaisses, épeurantes. Our rib cage rises pleasantly. We run notre main sur les os, proche de la peau. On frissonne at the feel of our own skeleton. Much as we desire thinness, we prefer the comfort of a fat insulated body. Perhaps the real function of "baby fat" is to swaddle the selves in portable amour maternelle. Woops. Maman descends du plafond blanc down — plunk — dans le bain avec nous. She straddles our belly. Her buttocks squeeze us to attention. Sa main droite tient notre menton & jerks notre tête forward. Elle s'accroche le focus drette entre nos yeux. Elle tire avec sa droite & pousse avec sa gauche. She blows fumée dans notre face.

"P'tite folle, sais-tu comment je t'aime? Ma vie est rien sans toi, vide."

& elle regarde. Meanwhile, we grip les cotés du bain so we won't be sucked into Maman's open vagina, gaping juste sous notre coeur. She claims us as une ancienne partie de son corps qu'elle veut reprendre. We tighten notre ventre & stiffen notre corps hard contre elle. We heave her off balance. Sa jambe gauche vole en l'air juste assez longtemps for us to

shove her back juste assez loin for me to slip out
from sous elle. Part of me doesn't make it, sucked
in, engulfed. In the bathroom's deux cent watt
starkness, my flat knee tops, skin blanc
promonitories against the tub's enamel-blanc, rise
from the soapy vanilla-icing-blanc. Deux glaciers
silver-blancs dialoguent over the sea suds. Pour un
moment, c'est cool & paisible. Je maintiens cet état
d'harmonie & nothingness by holding my breath.
My lungs burst. C'est elle, Maman, metamorphosed
into un poing punching mon diaphragme, I exhale
her & slowly blow out a million watts of lightning
zaps, noirs; sharp purple zigzags; & flashing spots,
rouges. Maman s'installe sur la toilette & croise sa
jambe, allume une cigarette, se soulève, jète
l'allumette in the toilet. Elle attend comme si elle
veut quelque chose de moi. Je dis, dans sa langue,
"Je vais t'écrire." Sa bouche twiste & elle dit, "C'est
pas la même chose." Ce qu'elle veut dire c'est: I
shouldn't go away. Ce que je veux dire c'est: I can't
wait to go. The family-size Ivory soap bar coasts on
wavelets of liquide tiède. Elle m'abandonne. Je
répète ses paroles, je les apprends par coeur:

"P'tite folle, sais-tu comment je t'aime? Ma vie est
rien sans toi, vide."

Les mots plaisent dans la bouche. Mots féminins.
Jeunesse. Promesse. Délicieux. I'll try it the other
way.

"Little fool, do you know how much I love you? My
life is nothing without you, empty."

The words slide off without taste or after-taste. But
they do it fast.

THE COUNTER

Wipe the counter.
Count the times.
One. The time
you asked, "I can call
your lover, can't I?"
The whites of your eyes
over easy.
Fries.
Bacon bits on your chin.
Cold toast
hardened and dried.

Two. The time
your eyes
— always eyes —
followed her away.
I paid the bill.
Tipped
generously.

Three.
And the time you said
"Don't stand near the wall,
the blood will spatter."
So I smashed the window,
a naked escape.
Glass, cuts, walls, mess
for you to wipe up.

O HOME ON THE RANGE

my pen rides
bare back
across blue lines
scribbles
to your charlie parker
bronco beat

unhinged
cupboard door
swings spatulas
flies whisks
rears to your
bucking tones

by geez
bebop girl
burn my toast
lick my jam
kick in
the kitchen
ceiling

giddy-up pony!
we're cooking

WE MAKE THE AIR

if ever you don't want me anymore

how i washed and filled the spice bottles
rubbed vaseline into your hard heels
more awkward things (my tired arm)
how you held my life
heavy in your lap

i squeeze your breasts
pull you open
inside photos of us slip out
     red cardinal in our tree   max the cat
yeah sharp too and hollow and blue don't stop

laundry
leaves
letters
lists
burn my head on your breast
i like being mean to you i say
same thing   you say

bury me with you, okay?
wouldn't mind
you say

eternity: a long locked look
legs dangling in blue nebula
red-as-a-cardinal dresses
up over our asses
no underwear
black-as-a-cat pubic patches dripping

onto Andromeda still
the mother-sucking mother-raging ones
it's okay you say
that's what everybody does

DIMANCHE APRÈS-MIDI

buried in the kitchen after mass
on a rainy sunday afternoon
I watch maman reach over
the back burner
quiet the boiling sugar
tap her round wooden spoon
my eyes shrink in the shiny kettle
mouth stretches   maman says
put away the butter
et le lait Carnation
pours *le sucre à crème* into a shallow
pan to harden and cool
while we nap
rain taps the window
pours down the eavestrough
I warm myself in Maman's round back
the chenille bedspread tickles
like the minnows who nibble
my legs by the dock
she grabs under my arms
hikes me up to her
reddening face
pas un mot
sprays my eyes closed
pas un mot
I wriggle
like the minnow on the hook
two round eyes make me
lie perfectly still
I pretend to sleep and
the fudge hardens in the pan
like the sandy beach
on a golden day
where transported by
the sweetness of courage
i dig for my life

Horizons blurring

HORIZONS BLURRING

Horizons blurring
I balance the cliff
edge, overlooking
a valley, curved ridge
from buttock to thigh,
a small place, far down.

Do I fall or fly?

I free float in mist
till gorge wall becomes
green sky, glide contained
contours into a rocky
rivulet,
paddle with bare hands
through silver white waves.

Flying trout scale an
invisible wall
of cries
and splashing
disharmony.
Navigating time,
I tread in one place
toward the centre
to the sea bottom.

Sky coalesces
a poem mirrored
in your urchin eyes.

SHADOW AND CLOCK

shadow: more than shade   butch

clock: iron hands

shadow: game of fingers a doorway a cigarette

clock: two arms   one busy one   one lazy one

shadow: does not exist   demarcates time

clock: tells time where to go

shadow: black of it   of the gazebo   where netting
           meets   blue sun   smacking it   face down
      flat   in grass

clock: face of eyes   watches

shadow: edges melting into a million ants

clock: wet leaves in the bed

shadow: paint the windows   soundless

clock: a chicken in the oven

shadow: hibernates   burrows   licks

shadow went inside and inquired of clock the
time   never you mind replied clock as she
climbed off her nail   stepped on the fridge

and rolled out the door   shadow and clock went for a walk and of this they did talk   the space behind the cupboard where things fall   the grasshopper who danced from shadow to light but never touched the line in between   the gap between the boards on the porch   the roots that freeze before they sprout   the leaves that redden in july   and shadow and clock confessed   they were both catholic   and both obedient   and mathematical   acrobatical   nautical

A SHADY DIAGONAL

270°W

    a well   a gorge   a bird
    three split logs
        voluminous silence
    a hook of queen anne's lace
    a bone of an arm
    crusty fingers paint
    the well-well-well of it
        bugs

    wind rustles poplars
    tissue-paper crisp
    the loveliness of sundays
    starched dresses and slips
    and the unsticking   unweaving
    of this lost world
        this thing

240°SW

    absent from where I am
    hat and sunglasses and moving pen
    perched in a lawn chair
    official observer and note taker
    scientific worker
    small snaps in tall grasses
        grey fractions

        love's imperfection
    crawling in my shadow
    traveling my profile
    itching nostrils
    brown-speckled
    earth breasts
        ant mounds

135°SE

    the smallness of the valley down each blade of grass
    air balloons at a country fair
    the largeness of the sky
    the curl of your head
        you can go to china on a cloud

    i ask you black-eyed susan
    i ask you red-leafed bush
    crackly tree   spider   rusty car
    shouldn't we be scrubbing clothes or baking bread
    or nursing?
    praising god or praying?
        is beauty of any use?

75°NE

    the creases in your felt hat
    corn husks
    the smell of raw eggs
    pine needles on the roof of my mouth
        blue milk

    i am in a rage
    you can tell by my serenity
    i am an arrow flying
    a baseball cuffed up and out
        a car running off the edge

345°NW

    sly comforts
    spit music   mint drink
    two porcupines in a tree
    calloused feet

tearing bark   cold legs
a pale nightgown

a wall of folding doors
        unfolding

the startling joy of a cold lake
the most beautiful tree
its trunk an upturned handle
like a swing it sits
in the dark it grows
in a swampiness it creaks
splits in three
subdivides again

dying and
        the beauty of it

THE ORDINARY HORNBY VIEW

Sea lion chorus
line, tails high kicking,
snouts surfacing, brown
torsos glide mauve sea.

City eyes count up
sea gulls, one hundred
at least, who
squawking mid-air, vacate
the glistening stones:
wrinkled grey foreheads
in a turquoise stream.

Cerebral eagles
widen square talons,
land and take off in
perpendicular
perfectionism,
clamping a beak full
of silver supper.

Levitating fish writhe,
last fling high flyers
fastened on icy winds.

The ordinary
Hornby view, for hours,
eyes the beholder.

ARISTAZABAL

by the creek
in rosy light
i kneel in high grass
to pay homage

nestled among billowing bulbs
her sultry trunk rises like aphrodite from verdant
                                             waves
(boisterous)
kicks up ruffled roots
sways in the wind

ambitious johnny jump-ups compete
purple and yellow
for her attention

the infinite magnetic circle of her queenly gaze
                                          ricochets
against my skin

knees up to my chest
toes wriggling in plush moss
the thrill of flirtation scurries through my own
                                       folded trunk
tugs my hair roots

rising moon winks prism-like diamond cascades
prickles my scalp

i slip my feet between curvaceous roots
wrap both arms around her
listen in silent contemplation
her melody shrieks
buzzes
lands on my lips which part to receive her rhythm
weaves around my tongue
and before i'm ready

penetrates my wind canal
tickles my diaphragm
scarlet hibiscus giggles at my feet
blue delphinium fingers vibrate my spinal vertebrae
i stand on tiptoe
scrape my chin along rough bark
swallow full throated her bitter sap
salty
like my own girlish perspiration
(sigh)

rational mind protests
you're hugging a tree
less rational now
you're hugging her tree

she and i covet trees with a circumference suitable
                                            for human arms
a rare treat on aristazabal
indeed in any rain forest

it started the night
she jolted me from a green afterglow
& pried out my secret
she got hooked too
& needed fresh greenery nightly

always i let her have the first embrace
just this once
i wanted to be number one

i retreat from her cold stare with a gesture that
                                         means
i m sorry
i m not really but i want to snap her out of this crazy
vengeful posture
visions of our original catastrophe haunt her day &
                                         night
& manifest in her breasts & loins & belly

in all her soft places
where weary bones frame a lurid still life of
                                          unsheathed
knives
heavy hands poisonous drool pulverizing fists

closer
i inch my hand to the rigid area between her ribs
she anticipates my touch
like a child preparing to catch a rolling ball
here it comes
her eyes lower
catch it now
she sucks in air
blows out
i make contact
at-a-girl

Dry-throated sky

LES BRAS CHAUDS

1.
Les bras chauds
de ta veste de laine
m'entourent.
J'ai les poches pleines
de mémoires.

Déjà, c'est un temps lointain.
Tu vivais là
a l'autre bout
du fil du telephone.

Déjà, c'est un pays étranger.
Tu vivotais, maladive,
avec esperance. Tu
avais un bon moral.

Mes joies regrèttent ta vie,
incomplète,
finie avant le temps,
sans cérémonie,
comme tu as vécue,
simple, vraie,
en douleur,
vite.

2.
Une pensée traverse
le jardin dans la pluie
et laisse de traces de boue
sur le plancher de cuisine.
Une pensée passe un sejour

THE WARM ARMS
Translated by Susan Kealey

1.
The warm arms
of your wool jacket
envelop me.
My pockets full
of memories.

Already, it's long ago.
You were there
at the other end
of the telephone line.

Already, it's a foreign country.
You struggled along, weak,
yet hopeful. You were
in good spirits.

My joys belie your life,
incomplete,
finished before its time,
without formalities,
just as you lived:
simply, honestly,
in pain,
quickly.

2.
A thought crosses
the garden in the rain,
tracks mud
on the kitchen floor.
A thought sojourns

sur le parterre du voisin
et éparpille des brins d'herbe
sur le tapis de salon.
Une pensée s'enfuit
par la porte d'en arrière.
Je cours après mais
elle disparrait.
La pensée revient. Je l'ignore.
Elle n'est pas rare, cette pensée,
elle aime à s'enfuir.

on the neighbour's lawn,
scatters blades of grass
on the living room rug.
A thought escapes
through the back door.
I run after it but
it disappears.
The thought returns. I ignore it.
It's familiar, this thought,
it enjoys running away.

EASTER

winter undresses

new white shoes
hop-scotch, hot step,
Lent's finale

(clickers)

lilac dress succumbs
over my hips
floats on crinoline clouds

sugar-crisp
like a dashboard doll

the sun melts
her marble eyes
searing hope
like a laser
into us.

DRY-THROATED SKY

Garden hose hisses
into my sleep,
explodes brown
feathers in the dew.

I emerge barefoot,
yawn steel air.
Limping cement paths
chip off, cling to chalky
heels and toes, heels and —

Snapdragon sentries
in pink-peach line-ups
deflect the daylight.
Velvet hollyhocks
blindfold the sun, clasp
with fibrous fingers
my outstretched hand,
mock my muffled moan.

Dry-throated sky
sucks clear underground,
to flesh beds, mother
bones, blue roots, tangled
memory mazes.
Tall dandelion
disintegrates one
more dream.

GRACE

    on a monday or a friday
    or any schoolday
    in nineteen fifty seven or eight

    at five thirty p.m. or so
    when it's dark
    and ten below

    in the name of
    her presto cooker
    her potato masher
    and her cutting board

    eat yellow beans
    eat baby carrots
    eat roast beef

    dip white bread
    into the broth
    tenderly amen

AFTER SUPPER

Winter's just over,
pa's left for the mine.
Just me and you, ma.

One smoke, one coffee,
one little minute
before you set up

the sewing machine.
Supper's just over,
sun's lingering and

old Cecile stops on
her way to bingo,
just sits for a laugh

invites you to go
along. You grumble.
Can't. Got to finish

her bed ruffle; dress
up her bedroom, eh?
And we both show off

the lacy fabric,
slide a hand over
two hundred percales.

Luminous cotton
meets pink sunset rays,
cigarette sparks

menace in the air
like the promise you
made me and keep
breaking.

DEATH SONG

    you're home she laughs

    i lift maman one
    arm beneath her knees

    scalp pink between white
    hair follicles
    indented temples
    transparent eyelids

    in the street below
    summer construction
    starts at five a.m.
    cement truck crumbles
    pavement

                      between each
    thin breath hard rock breaks

    a white masked cracker
    jack in buttoned white
    spats and bowler hat

        croons and soft shoes
                  death lounges backstage

    flesh bags her brittle
    knuckles like loose hose

    september seventh
    toronto phone rings
                  death swallows maman
                  whole
    dreambody knows first

    blood evaporates
                  death flicks a switch

BROTHER

Like turtle hatchlings,
gulls and owls looming,
scramble to the sea,

we run for our lives,
red tongues in the sand,
till eternity.

In a hard rock room,
cigarette ashes
drop into your beer.

You swallow ashes,
gesticulating,
behind the smoke screen.

Ancient woman, man,
swallowing, trembling,
immigrate, pack up

thick red earth chunks in
an old black suitcase.
A gift to you, child,

breast-fed discontent,
bitter milk, sour
red soil in our veins —

to drown out with booze,
to numb out with dope,
to sweat out with slog,

to smoke out, cry out,
piss out, vomit out,
blow out, move from the

inside to the out.

"For god's sake, brother,
why can't we do it?"

I want to ask. I
swallow a hard rock
in a hard rock room,

gesticulating.

COLLECT YOURSELF

    tighten stitches
    re-knit raw écru
    get the tension right
    hem satin slips
    lay our pearls   gloves
              straw plaited panama
                    sunday still life
                    a white chenille bed

    freeze dry
        violet   orchids
        hands   moons
    and behind frozen peas
        kisses so gentle you
    know not what to say
        or do
    but preserve the evidence
            keepsakes
            proof of a past

    visit the desert
        on a moonless night
    watch lantern light flicks
        on a canvas tent
    silhouette shadows
    tremble from within
    eye glasses   shatter
    red wine   spills
        on brown sand
        romanticize
        love in pain
        pull back
        get a better view

    visit the ocean

        a sun blind mission
        scour bleached beaches
        kneel among starfish
        and turtle eggs
            cracked
        by the morning tide
                dig up traces
                of ordinary
                colour deprived
                life

bury the remains
        dried blood
and shaking a round pan
sift from the gravel voices
        the golden grains
        the threads of
a woman alone

THE NORTHERN CLINIC

maman doesn't drive
papa is at work
so we have to get taken
like children
to the northern clinic

broken folding chairs stacked
up on the empty stage
maman and i sit
in the circle
wait
for our appointment
with the specialist
from six kids
(maman says)

my name gets called
finally
my name
mispronounced

we march past
braces
wheelchairs
stumps

behind the curtained
divider
free-standing
temporary room
portable x-ray
viewer dictating
machine

excuse my english
maman says
you speak very well

he says
he looks at x-rays
he looks at me
examines me
my incisions

my spine

a foot breathes
toes inhale

air blows out the toes

music waves
palm of the foot
heel
flat
stump

a foot breathes the earth

ten toes inhale earth
gliding

a wind lifts
earth inhales ten toes
a foot

what if the body took off
and the spirit stayed?

invisible
instead of
blind

absent

UPON A BROTHER'S DEATH

Your body stilled, your spirit enters me,
alights between my ribs, alive and free.
A hollow sound I hear, a sighing echo,
A soulful whisper speaks, *Hello, hello.*
My shoulders cave, my fingers rush to hold
my chest; you dance between my bones as bold
as life recalled. Arise, rekindled sprite,
and fly, escape to cast on high your tight
unwinding reel in arcs from sky to blue
of northern lakes. Astride a sloping rock,
inhale the rising sun, the morning dew.
If now I rest and so might you, we owe
to moments when, ignoring time's tick-tock,
you hooked a trout and grinned, *Hello, hello.*

About Lina Chartrand
June 10, 1948 - April 2, 1994

Lina Chartrand was an accomplished and prolific poet, writer, dramatist and screenwriter who is also remembered for her passionate commitment to social activism.

Lina was born in 1948 in the franco-Ontarian mining community of Timmins. After she contracted polio at 16 months, her childhood was marked by a series of operations. As a result, her mobility was affected throughout her life.

Lina lived with her parents in Timmins until she went to Queen's University in Kingston to study drama. In 1970, after receiving her B.A., Lina moved from Kingston to Toronto where she was active in a wide range of community organizations.

These included Crutch, a disabled people's rights organization, the South of St. Jamestown Tenants' Organization, the Federation of Metro Tenants' Associations, Parkdale Community Legal Services, Downtown Action, the Law Union of Ontario, the Family Benefits Work Group, Lesbian and Gay Pride Day Committee, the Simon Nkoli

Anti-Apartheid Committee and Tenants' Hotline. Lina also worked for several years as a fieldwork supervisor with the George Brown College community worker program.

In the early 1980s Lina helped create feminist performance pieces with Robin Belitsky Endres and the other members of Pelican Players Neighbourhood Theatre. Their theatrical event Holy Cow: A Goddess Bazaar was a full twelve hours long. The performance marathon culminated in Lina's appearance as the goddess Aphrodite: standing in a washtub, her scarred back fully lit, she slowly turned to face the audience with a radiant smile.

With Amanda Hale and Cynthia Grant, Lina cofounded The Company of Sirens, a feminist political troupe. With the Sirens, Lina wrote, developed, performed and fundraised for numerous scripts and productions, including The Working People's Picture Show.

Lina's collaboration with artist Amanda Hale led to a number of ground-breaking multidisciplinary performance pieces about female sexuality, some of which were presented at the Gay Sweatshop International Festival in England. These works include Switching Channels, Lost and Found and Private Parts, Public Parts.

For her poetry, drama, screenwriting and fiction, Lina drew upon the inspiration of her early life. Her screenplay French Kiss, and the draft of her novel of the same name, centre on a young Northern Ontario girl's search for independence. Another screenplay, Sister Claire's Holiday, explores the tender friendship between a nun and a homemaker in a small franco-Ontario Catholic community.

Lina's experience with polio, and her year as the young Miss Easter Seals in 1960, provided the themes of her bilingual play La P'tite Miss Easter Seals. La P'tite was mounted in 1988 by the Théâtre francais de Toronto, directed by John Van Burek at the DuMaurier Theatre, and published by Sudbury's Prise de Parole in 1993. An English language adaptation aired on CBC Radio's Morningside in 1990 and was mounted by the Company of Sirens at the Tarragon Theatre in 1993, under the direction of Cynthia Grant.

Increasingly recognized for her dramatic talents, Lina became an inspiration to other artists, as writer-in-residence at Théâtre francais and as a dramaturge to other playwrights including Helen Carmichael Porter and Ingrid MacDonald.

Lina saw several short film scripts to production. Under the artistic direction of Marushka Stankova, Lina's first script, *Princess Margaret*, premiered at a National Film Board workshop in 1988.

In 1993 Lina attended the Canadian Film Centre. As a resident of the film school she furthered her screenwriting credits to include *Windy*, a short fim which she also directed, and *In Limbo*, a script inspired by the life of her brother Yves, produced by the Centre and directed by Glen Brown.

In the last four years of her life, Lina explored creative writing with a group of women she had met through workshops and classes. Lina staged and directed three of the group's public reading events. Several of Lina's poems were published in literary magazines, including *Contemporary Verse 2*, *Pittsburgh Quarterly* and *Grain*.

After her death, a wide circle of friends and colleagues established the Lina Chartrand Poetry Award in honour of Lina's work as a poet. Administered annually by the *Contemporary Verse 2* collective in Winnipeg, this award recognizes the merit of an emerging Canadian woman poet.

In 1997, many of these same people donated the resources to produce this volume so that the insight and tenderness of Lina's poetry could be more widely known.
By Brian Conway with input from Cynthia Grant, Sandy Fox, Maureen Hynes and Kye Marshall.

About Lina Chartrand's Poetry

Although Lina worked in many genres, she held a special affection for poetry. "Poetry's the best!" she would often say — her shortcut way of acknowledging poetry's power to move us, and to make us recognize and relearn ourselves. Getting a poem accepted for publication delighted her as much as her larger successes.

As with all her writing, Lina worked seriously and consistently at her poetry, reading widely and carefully, paying special attention to the rhythms and forms of the poets she was studying. As she says in one of her long poems, "Meet desire,"
...so why be afraid?
(Because you need to write with rhythm,
count syllables,
be specific metaphoric poetic.)
Lina often liked to work within tight, formal structures, and would turn to the challenge of a specific form — such as the sonnet she uses for "Upon a Brother's Death" — to amplify the emotion of the subject. However, she also wrote extended imaginative pieces, like "Meet desire" or "A shady diagonal," in a kind of letting go that was as exploratory as it was celebratory.

In many of her poems, including the more narrative "Doctor Xiabo" and "After supper," she favours a breathtaking directness. She achieves this through a simplicity of diction, very short lines and the use of spare images to evoke a large category of emotion, memory or experience. She uses a similar tension of style in "Collect yourself," a meditation on the life of one of her aunts, layering significant details to summarize an entire lifetime. And in all her poems, Lina shows a special agility in closing the poem, leaving the reader with an unexpected yet satisfying emotional or perceptual turn.

One of the most distinctive aspects of Lina's voice in both her poetry and her prose is her bilingual work. We've included her French poem, "*Les bras chauds*," translated into English by Susan Kealey, and a bilingual prose poem, "A similée," which shows her ability to work simultaneously in both languages with amazing dexterity and wit.

When Ingrid MacDonald called me in early 1997 to ask if I'd work with her to collect and publish Lina's poems, we had two main sources to draw on: my own files of poems Lina had workshopped in our women writers' group and Lina's computer and paper files. Lina had formatted some poems into chapbook form: this collection of twelve or so poems was titled "we make the air" and was dedicated to her partner, Kye Marshall.

I compared and compiled these sources to arrive at this collection. Only one or two poems have been omitted, and these because it seemed that Lina had abandoned them as drafts, or "mined" images and lines from them for use in later poems. As she often tried several different forms for the same poetic material, some of our work was to decide which revision was the latest.

The collection is shaped into three sections: poems that deal with love and passion; those that, though usually about other subjects such as friendship or love, hold nature and landscapes as their imagistic focus; and those that reflect Lina's childhood and family, including her experience of her mother's and brother's deaths.

I tried to allow a certain "airiness," an echoing or complexity of themes and images among sections. I've corrected a few spelling errors, and in some cases decided to let stand a misspelling that seemed intentional. I made capitalizations and abbreviations consistent, except where it appears Lina wanted new, internal rules for a poem. In only one or two poems, such as "Horizons blurring," have I allowed myself to change the punctuation slightly to clarify a meaning. In all other respects — text, spacing, line breaks and titling — the poems remain as Lina wrote them.

Lina's poems present us with dreams, desires, memories and especially those everyday moments whose surfaces preoccupy us; but as she unwraps and re-crafts them, she reveals for us the questions at their core. In "The northern clinic," Lina asks:

what if the body took off
and the spirit stayed?

We offer this book as one way of keeping Lina's spirit present and visible.

Maureen Hynes, editor